PAUL KLEE

Katalin de Walterskirchen

PAUL KLEE

RIZZOLI
NEW YORK

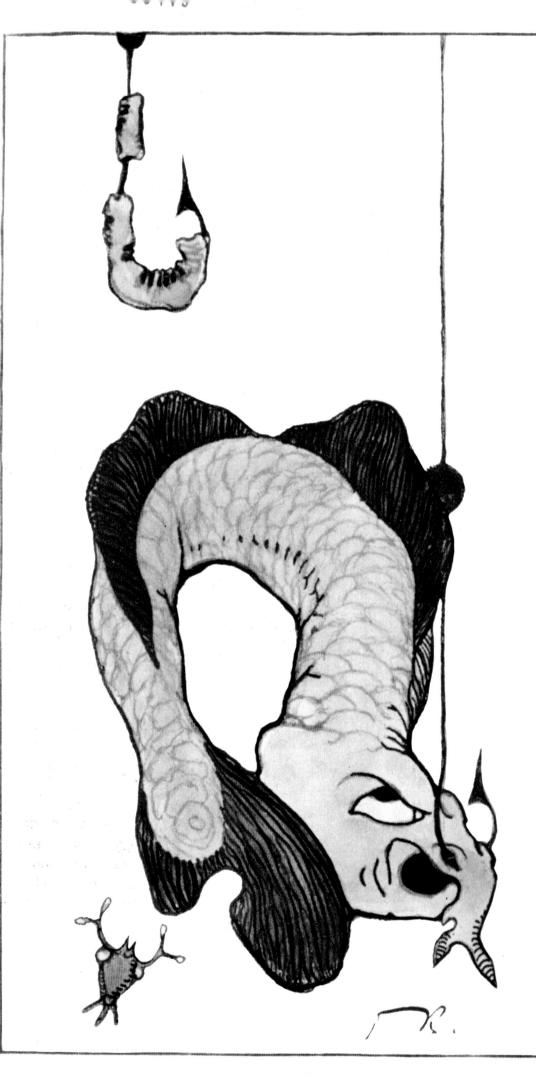

We thank the collectors
and museums that have given us their
assistance, among them: Bürgi, Belp;
Felix Klee, Bern; Kunstmuseum, Basle;
Kunstmuseum, Bern; Kunsthalle,
Hamburg; Paul Klee Foundation,
Kunstmuseum, Bern.

Photographs: Archives of the Paul
Klee Foundation, Felix Klee Archives,
Gérard Howald, Walter Klein, Jacob
Lauri, Meyer Erwin, Hubert de
Segonzac - *Paris Match,* and X.
Layout: Jacques Segard.

Double page 2/3 : Paul Klee in
his studio, 1925.
Page 4: Paul Klee, Dessau, 1933.
The works reproduced at the front of
the book are entitled:
pp 6/7: A Fish, Two Hooks, a Small
Animal, 1901. Watercolor and ink,
4.33" × 8";
pp 8/9: Meeting of Two Men, Each
Thinking the Other is More Highly
Placed, 1903.
(No. 5), etching on zinc.

Translated from the French
by Jack Altman

Rizzoli International Publications
712 Fifth Avenue, New York,
N.Y. 10019

French language edition:
© 1975 by E.P.I., Editions Filipacchi,
Paris, Cosmopress, Geneva, and
Spadem, Paris.
English translation published 1975 by
Rizzoli International Publications, Inc.
712 Fifth Avenue, New York, N.Y. 10019

Library of Congress Catalog Card
Number: 75-18525
ISBN: 0-8478-0007-5

Printed in France

The life and work of Paul Klee are characterized by his hunger for knowledge, comparable to Faust's, which fed as much on his real and imaginary environment as on the obsessions rooted in his artistic unconscious. But since he was not, like Faust, an alchemist or an initiate, he was not interested in the occult sciences, Klee did not reserve his knowledge for an elite of like-thinking people; he wanted to share it with a wide public through his works of art, his autobiographical writings and his academic art-teachings. Klee's art-teaching, as his biographer and interpreter Max Huggler so aptly observes, is practical and not speculative like that of his Bauhaus colleague, Kandinsky. Working from the fundamental elements of point, line, surface, and space (using light and shade), Klee develops a concept of three-dimensional graphics. On this basis he constructs a theory of color rooted in the Goethe tradition and enriched by Runge, Delacroix, Delaunay, and Kandinsky. A further essential part of his artistic theory—which Klee calls the study of structure of form—rests on the principle of the dynamics of artistic creation: "The work of art is born of movement, is itself movement fixed in space and is perceived through movement (the eye-muscles). (Klee: *Schöpferische Konfession,* Berlin 1920.) In this way, the conditions of creativity are presented. The technique of creativity is left to the practical ability of the artist. The technique finds expression in the preparation of the material on which the painting is to be made, in the mixture and application of colors, in the drawing-technique and in those effects peculiar to the artist. This tradition was nurtured mainly at the Bauhaus, where every art-teacher, including Klee, was at the same time head of a workshop and as such bore the title of "Master". Besides the means and techniques of creativity (which are never explicitly spelled out), Klee's art-teaching is to a considerable degree based on an original theory of composition. His aim is the "construction of unity through multiplicity" (Klee: *Bildnerisches Denken,* 1922), the regrouping of constituent parts within the work of art conceived as an entity. No work of art is a finished product, it is not a work that is, but fundamentally a work in the process of becoming. "The entity created by the artist must have a meaning in order to prevent art from being reduced to "pure formalism." In teaching his theory of art, Klee underlines this particular point: the analysis of the works of art operates on the basis of disciplines such as music, perspective, statics, mathematics, the natural sciences, philology, art history, literature, and philosophy. This teaching, based on practice and theory, speculation and empiricism, offers the key to understanding Klee and the complex vision of the world he wants to communicate to us through his work.

THE SHOW

Klee's life-goal was total vision of the world in which it is possible "to reconcile opposites, to express diversity in one word." One possibility of realizing this special goal expresses itself in Klee's constant attempt to reconcile opposing factors inherent in the cosmos, between the intangible microcosm and the unfathomable macrocosm. Apart from purely intellectual methods of explaining objective reality in its complexity, Klee uses another way, derived from the realm of emotion, in order to make his complex vision of the world comprehensible to the public: that of the theater. In the theater the dramatist projects the human psyche onto its environment and often at the same time reflects the character's environment through his actions. The actor's personality remains hidden from the audience, who can only perceive the character portrayed. This problem of the duality of man and mask is sublimated in the theater through the illusion of the action on the stage. Not so in the pictorial theater-world of Paul Klee. The unity of mask and actor is achieved in the comedian. Man's spirit merges with his outward appearance to become his true Self. Klee's theater pictures can therefore not be regarded as views of the stage: no play is required to understand his presentation. It is part of his view of the world, and since this is universal, it needs no addition of words or action.

Actor. 1923 (No. 27): Oil on paper 20"×10 1/2". He is standing before an empty stage. His forehead, with the brain hidden behind it (anatomical part of the personality) is separated from the mask-like face by a wide black head-band. The stiff gestures of this costumed character are those of a puppet. "The work is the reflection of the Ego," says Klee. Of the artist or of the observer?

☐ The numbers in parantheses in the captions of the works refer to the list drawn up by Paul Klee in the "catalogue raisonné" of his works which is the property of the Paul Klee Foundation in Bern. The "Works" notes are quoted from Will Grohmann and are specified in the Biography (p. 70). ☐

1923 // 27   Schauspieler

ctor. 1923.

The Spirits (Figures from a Ballet). 1922.

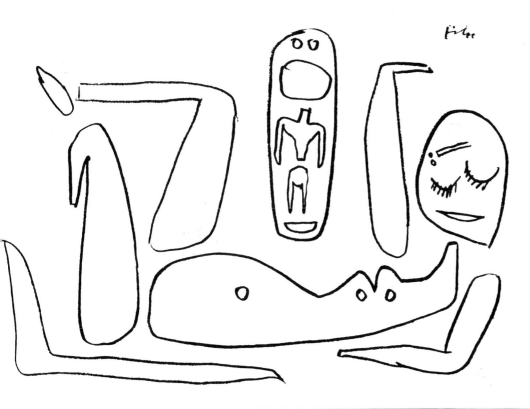

wn in Bed. 1937.

rits (figures from a ballet. 1922 (No. 122): Watercolor and pen on paper. 10" × 7". The composers Borodin and Moussorgsky tried to transform pictures into sic. Here Klee has done the opposite: he has translated sound impressions into an image. The figure in the foreground seems to represent the melody, the one ding modestly in the background the second voice, and the lively atmosphere of the stage the "accompaniment".

Clown in bed. 1937 (No. 254): distemper and tempera, paper on cardboard, 10 1/2"×11 1/4". It shows an artist in repose (one does not know whether he xhausted or merely enjoying some free time). No smile on his "unmasked" and vacant face. His soul depicted upper right (in a form that evokes a tuning-) scarcely has any relation to the body reclining on a cushion.

Duetto. 1929 (No. 332). Water-color, paper on cardboard 8 1/2"×13 1/4". Painted after a journey to Egypt. "Works of the Outer Circle."

Animals Play-acting. 1937.

The Singers' Music-Hall. 1930.

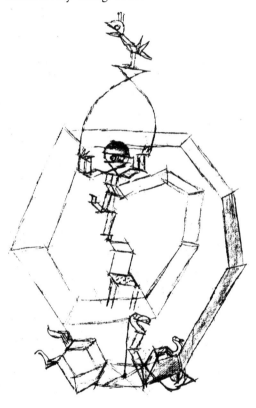

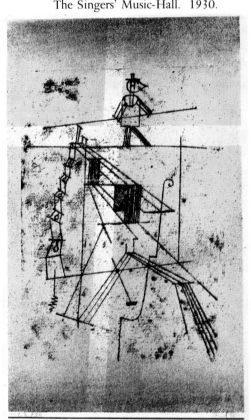

Rope Dancer. 1923.

The Timpanist. 1940.

The Animals play-acting. 1937 (No. 112): charcoal and red chalk on a tablecloth sprinkled with stars. 16"×16" Works: additions and new beginnings in Be
The Singers Music-hall. 1930 (No. 189): Watercolor on chalky base. On paper. 10 3/4"×19". Technical research: lace effects. "The dominant proportions c racterize the final form, the structures make the realization possible." (Klee).
Rope Dancer. 1923 (No. 138): color-retouched lithograph. 17 1/4"×11". Images, constructions. Works: absolute pictures.
The Timpanist. 1940 (No. 270): distemper, paper on cardboard. 13 1/2".×8 1/2". Is this picture of Klee his last self-portrait?

Bravura. 1939.

Carnival in the Mountain. 1924.

Dance of the red skirts. 1924.

Theater of Magic. 1923.

Bravura. 1939 (No. 1251): distemper and oil. Paper on jute. 39 3/4"×51". Late style of Bern: note the use of thick strokes. The figurative has become a hiero-glyph, symbolizing the beginning of World War Two in the form of a *danse macabre*.

Carnival in the mountains. 1924 (No. 114): Watercolor. Paper on cardboard. 10 1/4"×13".

Dance of the red skirts. 1924 (No. 119): Oil on paper. 13 1/4"×16 3/4". One of the Magic Pictures.

Theater of Magic. 1923 (No. 25): Indian ink and watercolor. Paper on cardboard. 13 1/4"×9". Technical researches: hatching.

ppet Show. 1923 (No. 21): Watercolor, paper on cardboard. 20 1/2"×14 3/4". Klee loved the theater. He had done some acting at the Bauhaus and he had often on puppet-shows at his home. The artist is recalling a childhood memory: The doll with a big head, frizzy hair and a heart-shaped body. In the background, to left, a window. To the right a unicorn, symbol of chilhood purity.

THE ANIMALS

Klee's work depicts a multiplicity of animals: camels, horses, vertebrates, females in gestation, but above all fish, birds, and snakes. Klee sensed the "animal essence" of beasts in the example of the domestic cat, and himself raised several splendid specimens: his paintings are imbued with their savage nature, their instinct for independence, coupled with their tendency to ingratiate themselves. Klee as artist and observer was especially interested in the animal as a form of life, part of the complexity of nature. Not that this would be the whole key to the secret of Klee's animal pictures. We begin to see the solution only when we recognize that the function of the animal in Klee's art is to represent the symbolism of the unconscious. How frequently we come across the bird-symbol of the soaring flight that Icarus dreamed of, the dream of detachment from the world. Again and again the snake appears, that mysterious reptile that tempted Adam and Eve, that enemy opposed by heroes of mythology, and the cause of man's downfall, the archetype for the release of the ego from the unconscious. Paul Klee's constant wrestling with the "spirit of Nature" is most evident in his paintings of fish, recurring through every period of his creativity. They are signs of his endless quest for his own place in the complex universe he envisioned.

The coming of the snake. 1939 (No. 1127): Distemper, paper on cardboard. 11 1/2×8 1/4". Its body comes from bottom right and moves towards the middle of the upper part of the picture. We cannot know exactly whether the head depicted is that of the snake or of a dreamer whose imagination the snake has invaded.

Concerning the archetype (primary universal perfect form), Klee used to explain to his pupils: "If one took the trouble, one could in some pictures interpret one or the other element by returning to the original form." He also said: "Even in the most abstract shapes one could still feel' the thread which leads to the archetype. That requires of course a specific experience. Occasionally the archetype of a form, even in an abstract rendering, can be discovered at first glance. Sometimes one discovers oneself in plants for instance. This process of osmosis (however limited it may be) is identical with St. Francis' statement that all creatures are brothers. This also applies to landscape. We are dealing with a new evaluation that includes water, land, air, clouds, stone, tree, animal, Man, machine."

e Coming of the Snake. 1939.

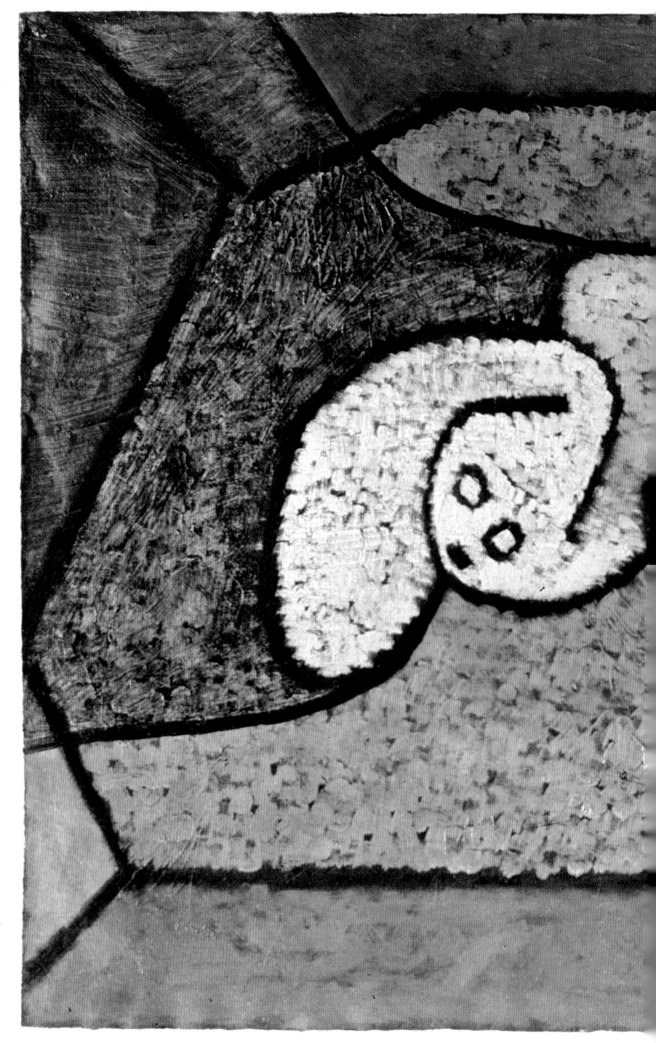

Four in their sleeping-place.
1939 (No. 388): Oil and watercolor on paper. 12 1/4"×19".

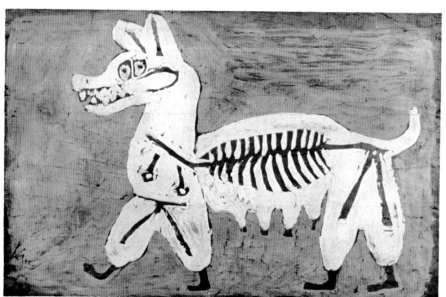

The Female. 1937.

Meeting of the Animals. 1938.

Woodlouse. 1940.

Woodlouse in Enclosure. 1940.

The Female. 1937 (No. 32): Oil, paper on cardboard. 8 1/4"×13".
Meeting of the animals. 1938 (No. 111): Oil on cardboard. 16 1/2×20".
Woodlouse. 1940 (No. 287): distemper on paper. 11 1/2"×16 1/4".
Woodlouse in enclosure. 1940 (No. 353): Pastel. Calico on cardboard.

Fish in a circle. 1926 (retouched in 1936—No. 140): Oil and tempera. Sized calico: 16 1/2"×17".

h in a Circle. 1926.

Bird Islands. 1921.

Red-wingend Marsh Hens. 1925.

Bird Islands. 1921 (No. 20): Drawing in oil and watercolor. Paper on cardboard. 12" × 18".
Red-winged Marsh-hens. 1925 (No. 108): Oil on paper. 8 3/4"×11 1/4".

Meeting of birds. 1918 (No. 202): Illustration for Lily Klee's guest-book. Indian ink and watercolor. 16"×3 1/4". Poem by Klee, 1902: " At the sight of a tree One envies the birds / They avoid / Thinking of trunk and roots / And self-complacently swing with agility the whole day long / And sing on the topmost branche

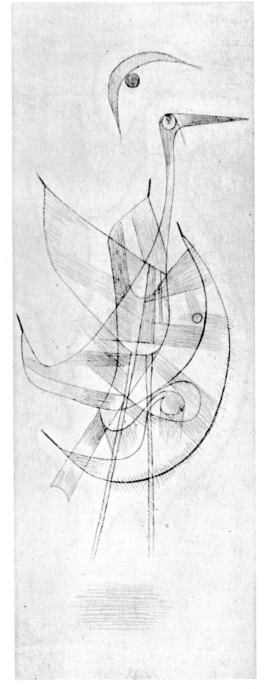

eting of the Birds. 1918.

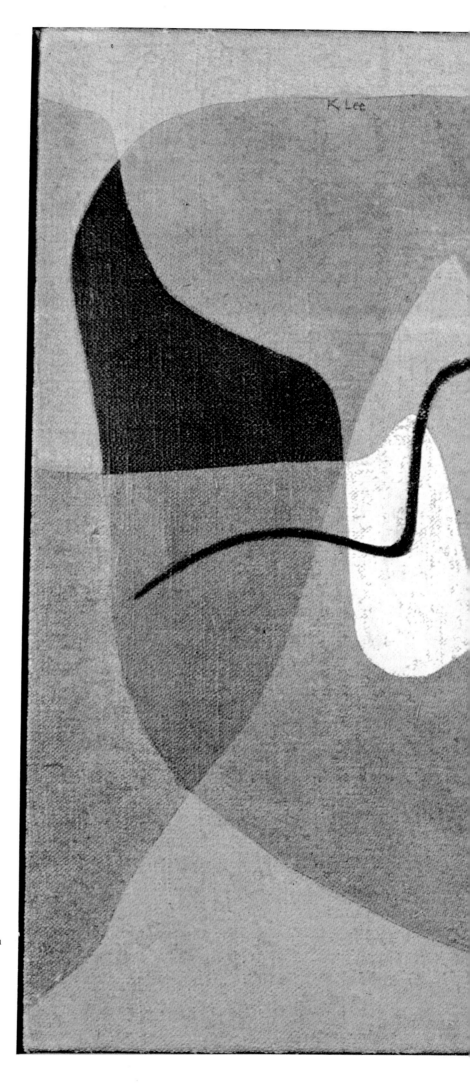

Snake Paths. 1934 (No. 217): waxed watercolor on stretched canvas, 16 3/4"×25".

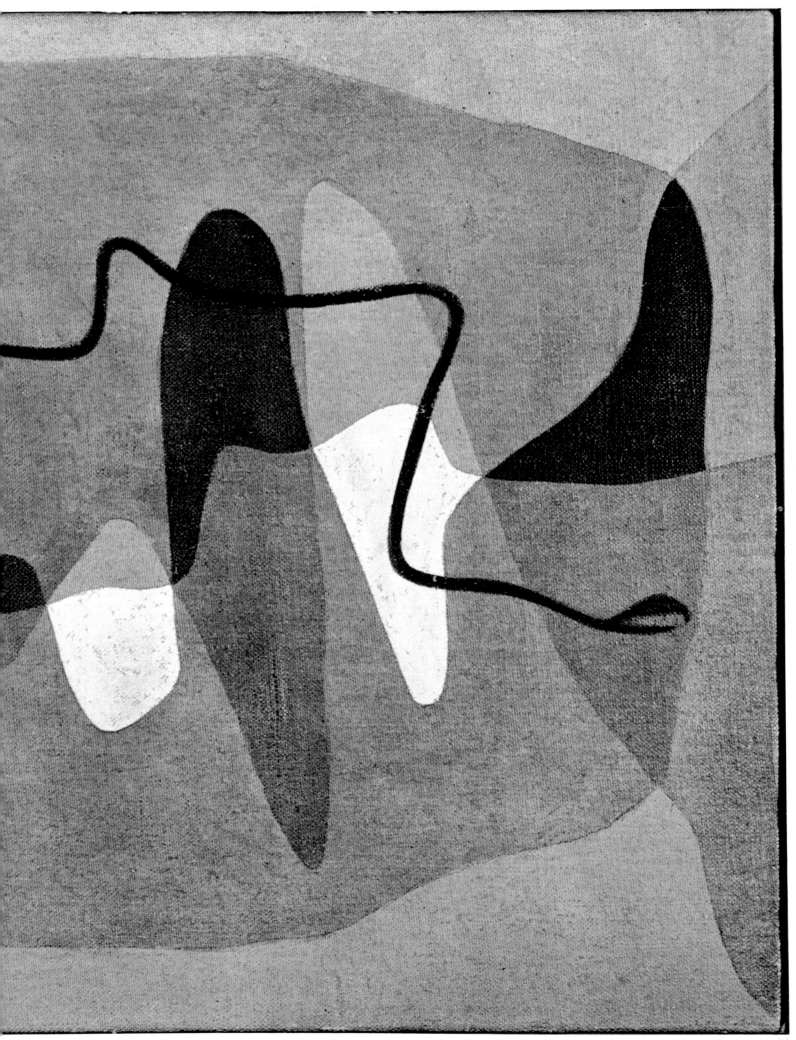

LIGHT

"Let there be light," according to biblical tradition, were the first words of the Creator, which is to say that without light, the eye—the most important of our senses—cannot perceive the physical world. For Klee the artist, who compared creativity in art to the act of Creation itself and who recognized his first and most imperative duty to be to "render visible," the problem of light was his principal concern. He knew from physics that sunlight is not monochromatic but like the colors in a rainbow. He took this into account in his theory of color and the treatment of light and shade. Thus light appears like a bundle in the atmosphere, either shaded or diffuse. In addition, artificial light has a different color effect than daylight has; the glow of fire is warmer than the reflected light of the moon. But Klee does not offer "a reproduction of the visible,"—he "renders visible." In those of his pictures that are divided up into several planes, he creates optical effects that evoke an "unearthly light," which would otherwise be invisible to the eye and reserved only for the contemplative spirit.

The Green church-steeple as a center. 1917 (No. 113): Watercolor. Chalky base on wood. 13"×10 1/4". The green steeple stands in the center, the illumination coming from bottom left. The visible and invisible effects of this encounter are presented to us in a complex ensemble: the eye moves along each line of color; a constant oscillation hints at the movement of the light-waves.

The Green Church-Steeple as Center. 1917.

Landscape in Blue and Orange. 1924.

Landscape near E. 1921.

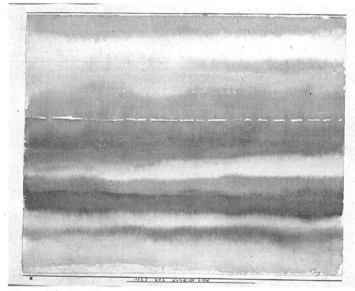

View of the North Sea. 1923.

Roof Terrace. 1932.

The Clearing. 1926.

Landscape near E. (in Bavaria). 1921 (No. 182): Oil, paper on cardboard.   19 3/4"×13 3/4".
Roof terrace. 1932 (no. 244): Watercolor, paper on cardboard.   19 1/4"×15 1/4".
Landscape in blue and orange. 1924 (No. 21): Oil, paper with chalk base on cardboard.   13 3/4"×19 1/2".   Klee shows a conflict with the chromatic circle; m̲
ment forms his basic principle, complementary colors evolving towards grey.   Klee calls it "complementary movement".
View of the North Sea. 1923 (No. 242): Watercolor, paper on cardboard.   At once natural vision and colored impression: a view of the sea where sky and water m̲
at the horizon.   The prismatic light of the sun falls on the landscape.   The diversification of colors gives a sensation of infinity.
The Clearing. 1926 (No. 118): Watercolor, paper on cardboard.   14 1/2"×20".   Klee has used here the whole spectrum of colors.   Three directions in the col̲
"peripheral", "diametral" and "polar towards white", to use Klee's terms in his Bauhaus classes.

it on Blue Ground. 1938.

uit on blue ground. 1938 (No. 130): distemper. Newsprint paper on jute. 22"×53 1/2". This large-scale painting, making technical use of fewer colors, is imbued
h the melancoly glow of a late summer heavy with fruit. A picture of maturity.

lowing two pages: **Fish-people.** 1927 (No. 11): oil and tempera, plaster and canvas on cardboard. 11 3/4"×20". Unusual presentation of an aquarium? We are not
*king with the perspective of men contemplating a fish but, on the contrary, with the perspective of a fish whose eye meets the inscrutable glance of the curious exa-
ning the underwater depths. Klee wants to give the observers of his picture the sensation of themselves being fish.

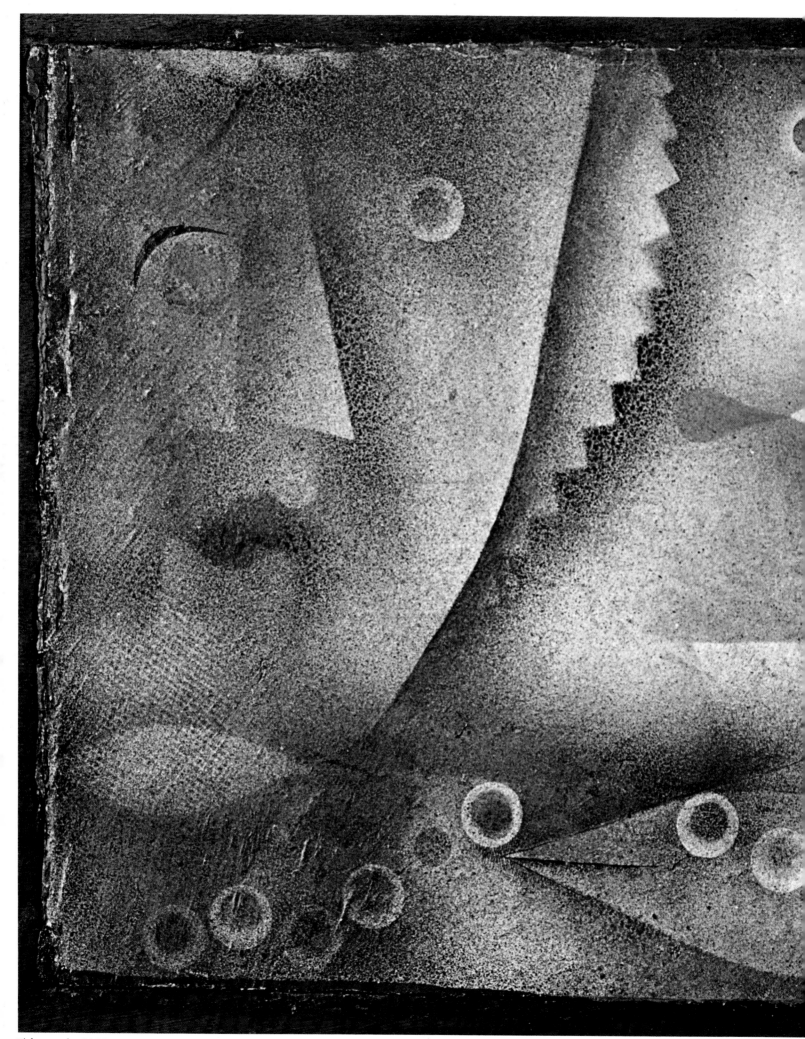

Fish-people. 1927

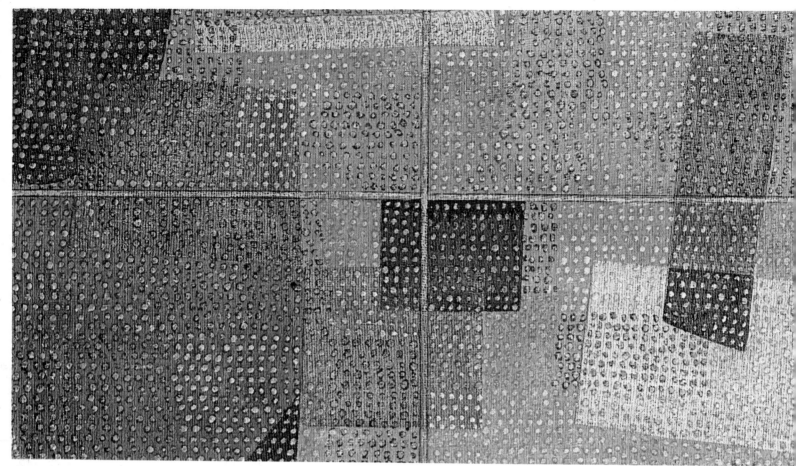

Through a Window. 1932.

Through a window. 1932 (No. 184): oil, gauze-covered cardboard. 11 3/4"×20 1/4". One of the Divisionist Paintings. The colors are infused with the gentlest brightness and transparency.

"**La Belle Jardinière**". 1939 (No. 1237). Tempera and oil on jute. 37 3/4"×28". In a hot and flickering open fire the memory of a beautiful gardener is conjured Her ghost, head bowed, balances a fruit dish in her left hand. During the time Klee lived in Bern, he did not work on his manuscript on artistic theory and we m therefore analyze his paintings. He probably used the color chart established by Max Planck *(Normtafel CIE 1931)*.

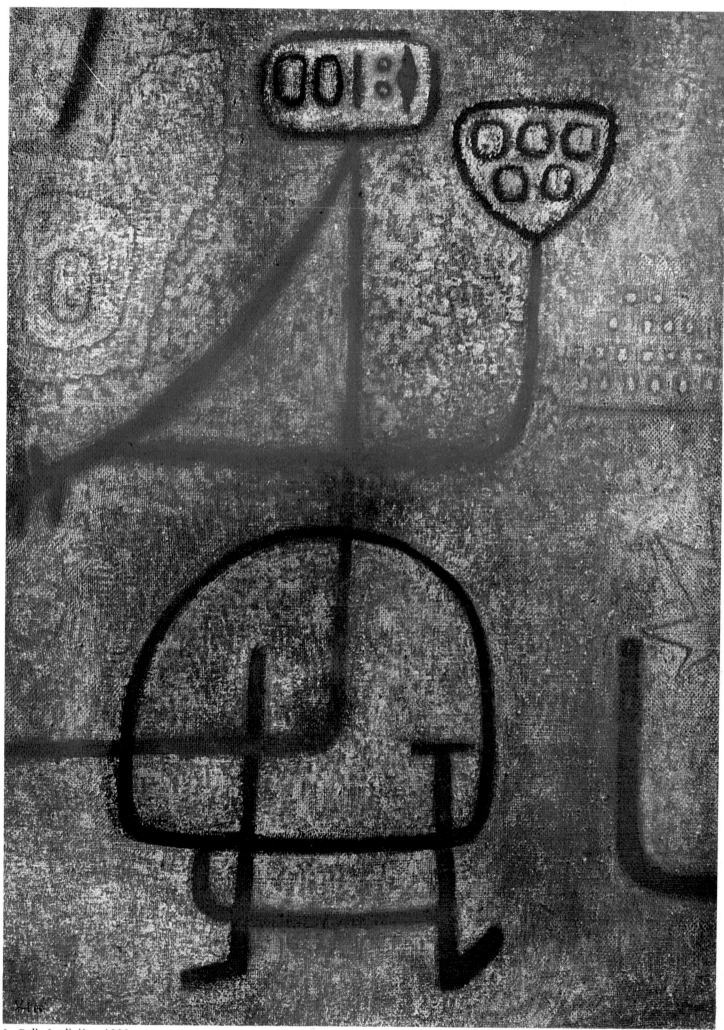

La Belle Jardinière. 1939.

Glass Facade. 1940.

The Goldfish. 1925.

Spring of Fire. 1938.

Glass façade. 1940 (No. 288): wax-color on jute. 27 1/2"×37 1/2". The light passing through this glass façade colors it in a way reminiscent of Klee's last still-
He experimented with the fixing of the pigments or their arrangement according to the twelve divisions of the chromatic circle of which he used slightly more t
half, that is to say, according to Klee, green, blue, violet-blue, violet, violet-red, red and red-orange.
The Goldfish. 1925 (No. 86): Oil and watercolor on paper. 19"×27". The burning warmth of the fish cannot be lessened by the surrounding sea. This "S
Marina" is the symbol of an ardent, inextinguishable love.
Source of fire. 1938 (No. 132): Oil, newsprint, paper on jute. 27 1/2"×59". "Oh fire-flower, you replace the sun at night / And shine deep into the silent hear
man." (Klee, 1900.)

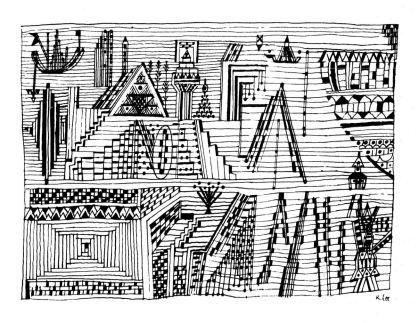

Sea Adventurer. 1927.

la Dulcamara. 1938.

Sea Adventurer. 1927 (No. 5): Watercolor on paper.   10"×12 3/4".   Work of the Outer Circle. Figures and landscapes.
la Dulcamara. 1938 (No. 481): Oil, newsprint paper on jute. 35"×69 1/4". Represents the luminous resting-place of the Ocean's dead.

Solitary. 1928.

Klee

ramid. 1934.

gratory Bird. 1926.

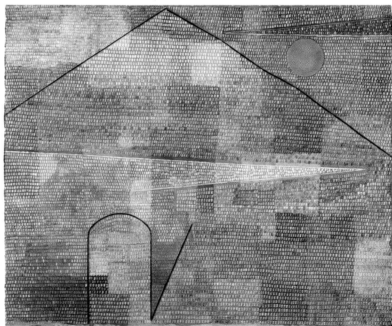

Ad Parnassum. 1932.

litary. 1928 (No. 80): Watercolor, paper on cardboard. 19 1/4"×9 1/2". One of the Atmospheric Compositions.

amid. 1934 (No. 41): Watercolor, calico on cardboard. 10 1/2"×17 3/4". Retrospective vision, influenced by Klee's stay in Egypt.

gratory Bird. 1926 (No. 218): Watercolor, blotting-paper on cardboard. 15 3/4"×19".

Parnassum. 1932 (No. 274): casein and oil on canvas. 39 1/2×49 1/4". The most important paintings using the same technique (that of the Divisionist Pictures)
: "Sunset", "The Light and a Few Things", "Landscape of Uol".

Small room in Venice. 1933 (No. 447): Pastel on ultramarine paper 8 1/4"×12". Works: unbroken intersecting lines. The deep luminous blue penetrates the picture as if from an external source. Polyphonic color.

The Moon was Waning and Revealed to Me the Grin of an Ill-Famed English Lord. 1918.

The Moon was waning an revealed to me the grin of an ill-famed English Lord. 1918 (No. 147): Watercolor, paper on cardboard. 6 3/4"×7 1/2". Tribute his friend, the poet Theodor Däubler.

Full Moon. 1927 (No. 23): Oil, cardboard coated with resin. 10"×12 1/2". In a rebus, there is no need for everything to be obvious! "You desire? / A glass ball What size? / Perhaps that of the full moon! / Smiles mutually understood. / Not everybody is endowed with understanding everything / I will suffer for it / and s then be betrayed." Klee, 1914.

l Moon. 1927.

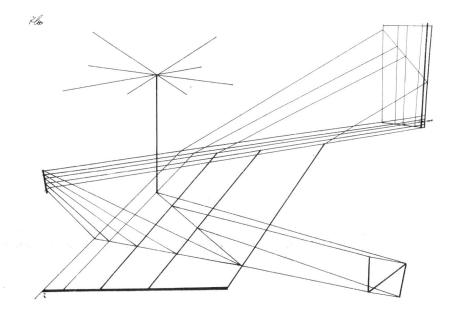

Marginem. 1930 (No. 210): Calculated according to what Klee called the "canon of colored totality" *(Kanon der farbigen Totalität,* Klee*).* Varnished gouache. ·dboard paper with base of white lacquer. 18"×14". "A symbol / The sun warms the mists that rise and fight against it." A poem by Klee, 1899. 31 years later y, Klee finally painted this vision. We see in it a fight between emerging life and the sun which gave it birth. The result is not yet known: it is difficult to deter-ne what has gained the upper hand and what has been vanquished.

STATICS
DYNAMICS

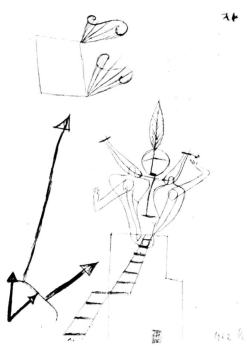

Klee's complex vision of the world is based on the principle that the cosmos is manifest not only as a phenomenon but that the individual elements of the cosmos stand in relationships to each other that are both diverse and constantly changing. In Klee's work, this becomes the problem of statics and dynamics. Dynamics must be understood in the context of physics: as a theory of those forces that create movement, but metaphysical components must be taken into account, such as the dynamics of becoming, created by the life-force, and the dynamic of acquiring knowledge in the human psyche, a dynamic created by the force of intellect. Statics, on the other hand, is the theory of the balance of forces which mutually cancel each other out. Even the arrow, that hieroglyph of velocity that is so often to be found in his work, is derived by Klee from physics. For Klee, the arrow represents at once force and movement, and this concept is not limited to physical and mechanical factors, a theory already expressed by Leibniz in his "*Discours de métaphysique.*" But even where Klee's pictorial world seeks balance and forces that lead to harmony of movement, one cannot forget the artist's demand that "Form must be linked with the concept of movement." Looked at this way, emphasizing the dynamic within the static and conveying static elements in a dynamic process, are constants in Klee's work, repeatedly found in his complex interpretation of the universe.

Conqueror. 1930 (No. 130): Watercolor, canvas on cardboard. 15 1/2×13 1/2. This is surely Klee's most dynamic work. The silhouette, tiny in comparison with the huge lamp which it is holding, surges forward. The head turned back for an instant, he runs (attacking or pursued?) towards a target of which he alone is aware.

nqueror. 1930.

Project. 1938 (No. 126): distemper paste, newsprint on jute. 29 1/2" × 44". At a psychological level the subject is a hieroglyphic composition. The dark part represents the subconscious and the bright part the conscious, that is to say what is perceived by the eye, ear, touch and smell.

The Wind of Roses. 1922.

Incandescent Landscape. 1930.

The wind of roses. 1922 (No. 39); Oil on Dutch paper. 16 1/2"×19".

Incandescent Landscape. 1930 (No. 242): Watercolor on red gum base, paper on cardboard. 8 1/4"×13".

Unstable Equilibrium. 1922 (No. 159): Watercolor, paper on cardboard. 13 1/2"×7". Klee also entitled it: "Activity in the Balance". "A little drama of the ho zontal, the scaffolding is vacillating... One can imagine that the force likely to provoke the fall finds its expression in the arrow and its measure in the weight." (Kl

54

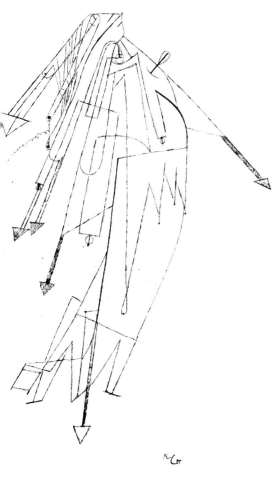

Unstable Equilibrium. 1922.

The Invention. 1934.

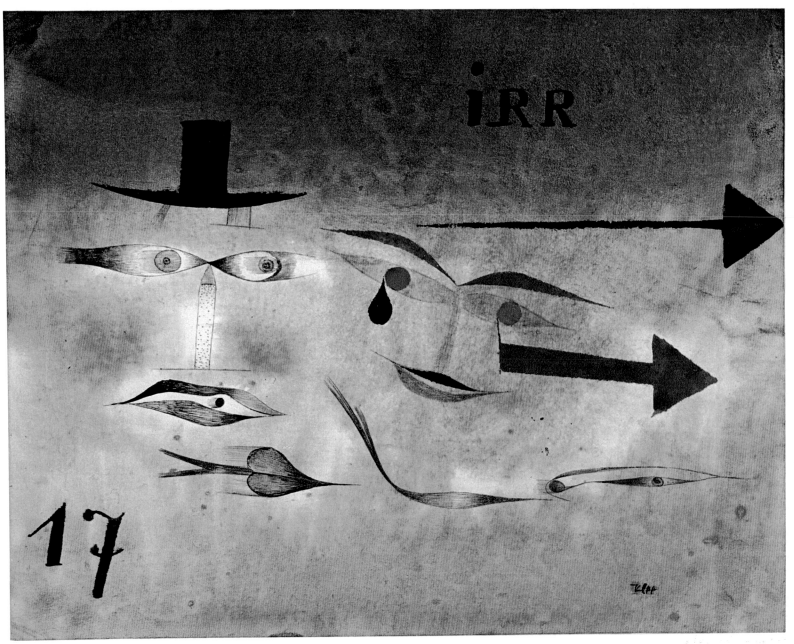

Seventeen-Irr. 1923.

Invention. 1934 (No. 200): painting in water varnished and coated with wax, on calico-covered plywood. 20"×19 3/4". Painted in Bern.

enteen-*Irr*. 1923 (No. 136): Pen and watercolor on paper. This picture was exhibited in 1925 at the Galerie Vavin-Raspail in Paris. Two masks are seen : one its mouth turned to the right with an eye looking in the same direction; the other, at an angle, pointed to the right, seems to be a woman at once joyous and lened: she is laughing and crying at the same time. The number "17" (age of adolescence) close to the word "*IRR*" (mad) seemingly leads us to the supposition this picture might satirize "mad youth".

wing two pages: **Fugue in red.** 1921 (No. 69): Watercolor on paper. 9 3/4"×14 3/4". A rhythmic structure in relation to light. As in a Bach fugue, repetitive nents appear in the composition, increasing and decreasing in movement.

Fugue in Red. 1921.

THE BEYOND

Only after grasping what is transcendental, what lies hidden in the sphere of methaphysics beyond rational comprehension, can one understand a non-material universe. The intermediaries of transcendence and the divine sphere were the angels, and Klee also makes use of them especially in his last years. Who could be better at conveying the incomprehensible to the ignorant than those spirits conceived to play the role of intermediary? In Klee's work they announce to us the end, the relief of long suffering, the growth of the spirit in the struggle between Good and Evil. Man stands in the center of this field of tension. He wants to experience the world in its complexity and fullness, he searches for what philosophers of all the ages have called Truth. In this search there are two irrefutable facts: Birth and Death, which make all men equal. Klee sees himself as observer and conveyor of this knowledge. He calls himself "I, Crystal" (Diaries 1915) and is referring to the sparkling reflection of the cosmic spectrum through eternally harmonious form —he is intermediary and takes on the role he had given the angel. He is an angel, that is, conveying the message of his complex vision to the world.

Poor Angel. 1939 (No. 854): Watercolor and tempera. Newspaper on cardboard, 19" × 13".

r Angel. 1939.

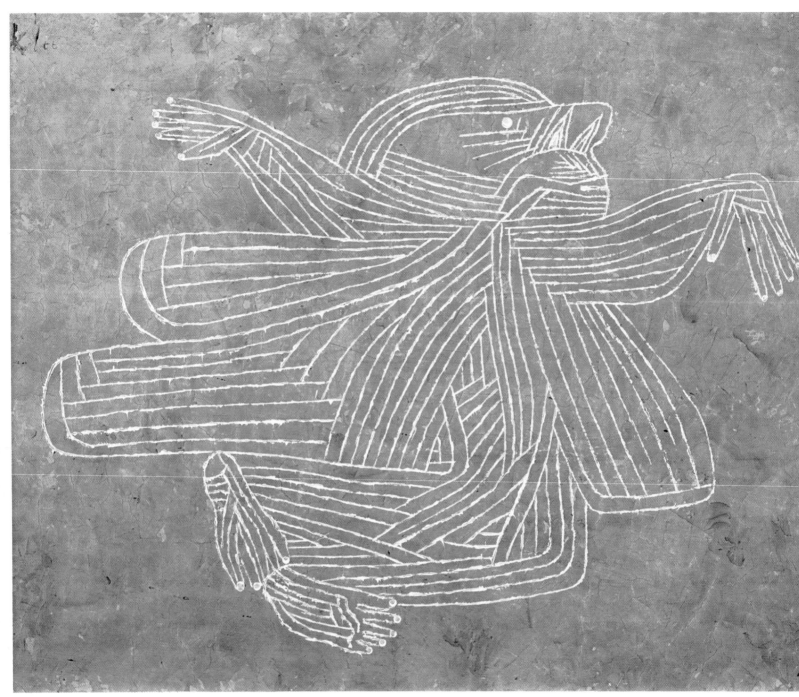

The Creator. 1934.

The Creator. 1934 (No. 213): Oil, stretched canvas. 16 1/2"X20 3/4". The Godhead, arms spread wide and garments flowing, hovers in the Cosmos which, His will, is illuminated by that first light. The space is entirely filled by the Creator whose white outline, powerfully executed, recalls Michelangelo of the Sistine Chapel. One knows that the spirit of God hovers over the waters. One feels the fresh pink light emanating from Him to spread over the world.

Angel Overburdened. 1939.

High Watchman. 1940.

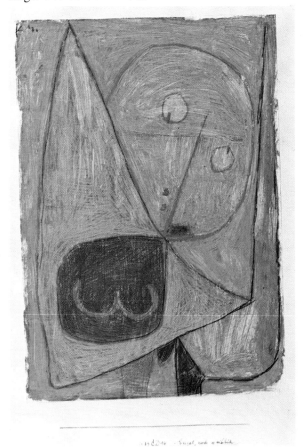

Angel still Female. 1939.

Angel drinking. 1930.

Angel overburdened. September 1939 (No. 896): watercolor on Japanese vellum. 20 3/4"×14 1/2".
Angel still female. 1939 (No. 1016): wax-chalk, paper on cardboard. 16 1/4"×11 1/2".
High Watchman. 1940 (No. 257): wax-paint on canvas. 27 1/2"×19 3/4".
Angel drinking. 1930 (No. 239): watercolor on paper. 19" × 12".

"...philosophize about death not out of resignation but in a quest for perfection." (Klee.) Even the Angels, who are immortal, seek in Klee's conception the perfection of High Watchmann. It is through this effort of ascent that they fall, take to drink, become unhappy, or retain a female form.

Temptation. 1934 (No. 12): Watercolor and distemper, paper on cardboard. 12 1/2" X19 1/4". The struggle with the forces of imperfection once more, this time represented by an angel (on the left) fighting the snake.

Head of Blue Devil. 1933.

Daemonia. 1939.

St George. 1936.

The Angel of Death. 1940.

Head of blue devil. 1933 (No. 285): Gouache covered with wax and underlined by plaster with gauze. 11 1/2×9 1/4".
Daemonia. 1939 (No. 897): Tempera and watercolor, paper on cardboard. 8" × 13".
Saint George. 1936 (No. 21): Oil, egg-tempera and watercolor on cardboard. 12 1/2"×17". It is man himself who, like St. George, must defend himself again
the savage red and green dragon.
The Angel of death. 1940 (Not listed in the catalogue of Klee's works): pastel varnished. 20"×26 1/4". The Angel will decide who is destined to die.

Death and Fire. 1940.

Death and Fire. 1940 (No. 332): Oil, distemper, jute on canvas. 18"×17 1/4". This composition, which Klee created in the knowledge of his imminent death, shows a silhouette approaching in the background and a death's head in the foreground dominates the whole. It belongs to a skeleton emerging from the earth. The risen dead wears a gold ring on his right hand, with which he seeks to attract the attention of the moving silhouette that is passing through the fire of life.

The man of fire. 1930 (No. 193): Watercolor on paper. 1 1/4"×8 3/4". He is not an angel but what an angel might see: the demon of fire, just emerging from an abyss, his head in flames and arms spread. His look shows envy of the world above him.

BIOGRAPHY

1879	:	December 18, birth of Paul Klee at Münchenbuchsee near Bern.
1886-1898	:	Primary and high school in Bern. Graduation, violin lessons.
1898-1899	:	Studies in Munich with Heinrich Knirr and in the studio of Franz von Stuck.
1899	:	First self-portrait.
1901-1902	:	First journey to Italy, particularly to Rome. Return to Bern.
1903	:	First etchings.
1905	:	First journey to Paris, visits the Louvre and goes to the Salon d'Automne to see the Fauves. First glass paintings.
1906	:	Klee marries the pianist Lily Stumpf. They make their home in Munich.
1906-1913	:	Devotes himself principally to drawing.
1907	:	November 30, birth of his son Felix Paul.
1908	:	Visits the Van Gogh exhibition.
1911	:	Illustrations for Voltaire's "Candide". Klee meets Kandinsky and Franz Marc. Becomes a member of the *Blaue Reiter*.
1912	:	Exhibits with the show of the *Blaue Reiter* et Hans Goltz's gallery in Munich. Second journey to Paris. Goes to see Delaunay and translates his essay "On light" for the magazine *Sturm*. Visits D. H. Kahnweiler, becomes acquainted with the work of Derain, Vlaminck, Picasso. At the gallery of Bernheim Jeune he sees pictures by Matisse.
1914	:	Visit to Tunis and Kairouan with Louis Moilliet and August Macke.
1914-1951	:	Kairouan watercolors. Cubism and Orphism.
1915	:	Host to Rainer Maria Rilke.
1916	:	First cosmic pictures (up to 1920). New forms.
1919	:	Munich. Experiments in oil-drawing.
1920	:	362 works exhibited in Munich at Hans Goltz. He is given a chair at the Bauhaus. Essay: *Schöpferische Konfession*.
1921	:	Moves to Weimar.
1921-1925	:	—Works of the Outer Circle: heads and figures, landscapes and still-lifes. Poetry, humor and satire. Poetry in a stricter form. —Works: Constructed and Absolute Images approaching the symbolic. Fugues, perspectives and compositions dealing with themes of opera and theater.
1922	:	Essay: "Ways of Nature Study" (*Wege des Naturstudiums*).
1923	:	Bauhaus exhibition in Weimar. Visit to the island of Baltrum. —First Magic and Musical Paintings (organized on the basis of rectangles). —Works: Technical inventions (hatching, stripes, screens).
1924	:	Speech to the Jena *Kunstverein* (Art Association). First exhibition in the United States. Holiday in Sicily. Closing of the Bauhaus in Weimar. —Works: Technical researches, lace-effects.
1925	:	Reopening of the Bauhaus at Dessau. 214 works exhibited at Hans Goltz in Munich. Participation in the first collective exhibition of the Surrealists in Paris. Exhibition at the Galerie Vavin-Raspail with a presentation by Louis Aragon. —Works: pulverisations.
1926-1930	:	Settles in Dessau. Journey to Italy. —Researches with parallel motifs recalling engraving.
1927	:	Journey to Hyères, Porquerolles and Corsica. —Researches with unbroken, intersecting lines (up to 1932). —Researches with distended surfaces and mobile bodies in space.
1928-1929	:	Journey to Brittany. Gropius leaves the Bauhaus. From December 17, 1928 to January 17, 1929, visit to Egypt. Exhibition at Flechtheim gallery in Berlin. Journey to Carcassonne, Bayonne, in the Gulf of Gascony. —Works of Outer Circle: figures, landscapes and still-lifes, atmospheric compositions, picture influenced by Egypt (beginning of the monumental style). —Script pictures.
1930	:	Several exhibitions in New York, Dresden, Düsseldorf, Saarbrücken, Bern. —Divisionist pictures: figures in stricter form, metaphysical spirit.
1931	:	Professorship at Düsseldorf. Journey to Sicily.
1932	:	Journey to Venice via Bern. The Bauhaus closes in Dessau and moves to Berlin.
1933	:	Break-up of the Bauhaus. Brief vacation on the island of Port-Cros. In December Klee move back to Bern.
1934-1940	:	—Late style of Bern: Technique of thick contours. —Series of works influenced by his stay in Egypt.
1936	:	Outbreak of his illness: scleroderma (hardening of the skin).
1937	:	Picasso visits Bern. —Works: Reminiscence of known styles.
1938	:	Pastels, the Tragic and the Demonic pictures, premonition of death, Angel series.
1939	:	Style before death. He painted and drew 1,253 works that year. Georges Braque visits Bern
1940	:	June 29, Klee dies at Muralto-Locarno.

Inauguration of the Bauhaus at Dessau. From left to right: Kandinsky, Nina Kandinsky, Mucha, Klee, Gropius, December 1926.

BIBLIOGRAPHY

Will Grohmann, **Paul Klee**, with a bibliography by Hannah Muller-Applebaum, librarian at the Museum of Modern Art, Abrams, New York, 1967.
Paul Klee: Supplement to the bibliography of Hannah Muller-Applebaum by Max Huggler. Published in the "Künstlerlexikon der Schweiz, XX Jahrhundert", Edition Huber, Frauenfeld, 1958-1961.
Paul Klee, fino al Bauhaus: catalogue of the Parma exhibition (November 7, 1972 to January 7, 1973), by Arturo Carlo Quintavalle, with bibliography. Published by the University of Parma, Instituto di Storia dell'Arte.
Denys Chevalier, **Paul Klee**, Flammarion, Paris and Munich, 1971.
Christian Geelhaar, **Paul Klee and the Bauhaus**, New York Graphic Society, New York, 1973.
Paul Klee, Handzeichnungen I. Kindheit bis 1920, by Jurg Spiller, Schwabe Verlag, Basel-Stuttgart, 1970.

Works of Paul Klee recently published:
The notebooks of Paul Klee. Volume I: **The Thinking Eye,** edited by Jurg Spiller, Wittenborn, New York, 1973.
Volume II: **The Nature of Nature,** edited by Jurg Spiller and Bernard Karpel, Wittenborn, New York, 1973.

Paul Klee with a white sports-cap (first self-portrait—black lead-pencil, 1899).

« *Traum*
Ich finde mein Haus : leer,
ausgetrunken den Wein,
abgegraben den Strom,
entwendet mein Nacktes,-
gelöscht die Grabschrift.
Weiss in Weiss ! »

(Tagebücher, Klee. Kap. 946)

PAUL KLEE

Katalin de Walterskirchen

Among the greatest achievements of twentieth-century art, the paintings of Paul Klee are examined in this beautiful book by one of Klee's most distinguished interpreters, Katalin de Walterskirchen, Curator of the Paul Klee Foundation in Bern. In her illuminating text and descriptive captions, the author offers fresh insights into the mysteries of Klee's art, an art that is complex, elusive, deceptively simple. Klee himself had a gift for poetic insight and interpretations; he was both theoretician and mystic, and his writings reveal a practical, carefully thought out approach to style and technique. His investigations into the problems of light, space, and movement resulted in a body of work that displays a dazzling variety of techniques, a rich inventiveness that bears the unmistakable stamp of genius.

But there is more to Klee than stylistic genius. His vision of the world was complex: dreams, symbols, the unconscious, imagination, nature—all contributed to his art. Analyzing the images Klee used, the author brilliantly interprets their meaning in the life and work of the artist. The 53 magnificent color plates and black-and-white illustrations enhance our view of the totality of Klee's work and permit us to share in the artist's belief that "art does not reproduce the visible; it renders visible."

RIZZOLI
INTERNATIONAL
PUBLICATIONS, INC.

New York

Printed in France

ISBN: 0-8478-0007